Many people believe that it is necessary to go into the countryside to find wild life. As you will see by reading this book there is a great variety of animals, birds, insects and flowers to be discovered, even in the heart of our biggest towns and cities.

Acknowledgments:
The publishers wish to thank Audley Money-Kyrle for the picture of holly on page 13 and M. M. Whitehead for the picture of a kestrel on page 46 and the picture of a house spider on page 39.
The following transparencies have been supplied by The Natural History Photographic Society:
the bat on page 32 photographed by Brian Hawkes
the mole on page 32 photographed by Stephen Dalton
the black ant on page 35 photographed by N. A. Callow
the great tit on page 42 photographed by E. A. Janes
the blue tit on page 42 photographed by A. Barnes
the carrion crow on page 44 photographed by Joe B. Blossom.

Nature in the Town

Written and photographed by Harry Stanton

Illustrations by Christine Owen

Ladybird Books Loughborough

Trees and Fungi

Horse Chestnut

The horse chestnut is easily recognised; during the winter the horseshoe-shaped leaf scar can be seen on the twigs.

In the spring the sticky buds burst into the large compound leaves with five or seven leaflets, followed by candles of white flowers. The nuts, which have a prickly shell, are called conkers.

▷

▽

Oak

Some oak trees are known to be over seven hundred years old and they may grow to be as much as forty metres high. The wood used to be used to build ships and houses but now it is used mainly for furniture. The bark is very thick and rough. The fruit of the oak is the acorn.

▽

Ash

A tall tree growing up to twenty five metres tall with a grey, grooved trunk. The wood of ash trees is valuable as it does not splinter and is used for the rungs of ladders, tool handles and hockey sticks. The seeds, called keys, have a wing at the end.

Plane

This tree is planted in towns and cities because it can live in the sooty atmosphere. The tree can be easily recognised by the bark which peels off in large patches, leaving yellowish patches underneath. The hanging balls of hairy fruits hang on the trees throughout the winter.

Privet △

One of the most common front hedge bushes. When allowed to grow, the white flowers have a strong scent. The privet and the ash are both related to the olive tree.

Laburnum △

The laburnum is not a native tree, but it is grown in gardens in towns and cities. The seed pods are very poisonous and must not be ◁ touched.

Hawthorn or May Tree ▷

A very quick-growing plant, which has red or white flowers, is used for hedges and as an ornamental tree. ▽

▽

Yew

The yew can live for over one thousand years. The tree is often found in church yards. Birds eat the red berries, but they are very poisonous to humans.

The wood is sometimes used to make fine furniture. Once it was used to make bows for archers. ▽

Lombardy Poplar

The Lombardy Poplar comes from Italy. It is a very quick growing tree often reaching over thirty metres high. ▽

△

△

Lime

This tree is often planted along roads in towns because of its beautiful heart-shaped leaves. The trees can live for over one hundred and fifty years and if not pruned can grow to over thirty seven metres high. ▷

The Wheatley (or Smooth-leaved) Elm is identified by its leaves, which are smooth and smaller than those of the more common Wych Elm. It also has a narrower top.

Elm

Many elm trees in Britain are dying from a disease called Dutch Elm disease. The elm is a very tall tree with a deeply fissured bark. It can grow to over thirty seven metres in one hundred years . Elm wood has a beautiful grain and can be used to make furniture.

Silver Birch

A native tree of the British Isles, it is a decorative tree and planted in gardens. Perhaps easily recognised by its peeling bark. The wood is used to make chairs and toys.

▽

▽

△

Weeping Willow

△

There are several types of willow. The weeping willow is often planted in gardens as an ornamental tree. It lives for about fifty years.

Sycamore

Although it lives for less than two hundred years the sycamore is a tall tree with a thick trunk. The wood can be used for flooring and for the backs and sides of violins.

Beech

Beech trees can have enormous trunks – over nine metres around – and large, smooth grey branches. In the dark shade of the beech very few other plants can grow. The wood is very hard and is used to make furniture.

Wild Rose △

Often found in hedges, in autumn this plant has bright red fruit called hips. Hips can be used to make wine and jam. ▷

◁ *Elder*

The name Elder is derived from the Anglo Saxon word meaning 'hollow tree', because the wood contains a white pith which can be easily hollowed out.

▽

Hollow elder twigs have been used throughout history to make toys such as whistles and peashooters.

The flowers, which appear in June, form heavy clusters and have a strong fragrance. The berries, which can be seen in September, are purple-black.

Crab Apple

A tree with a rough bark. The apples are bitter but they can be used to make crab apple jelly. The wood is very hard and at one time was used to make mallets for wood and stone carvers. ▽

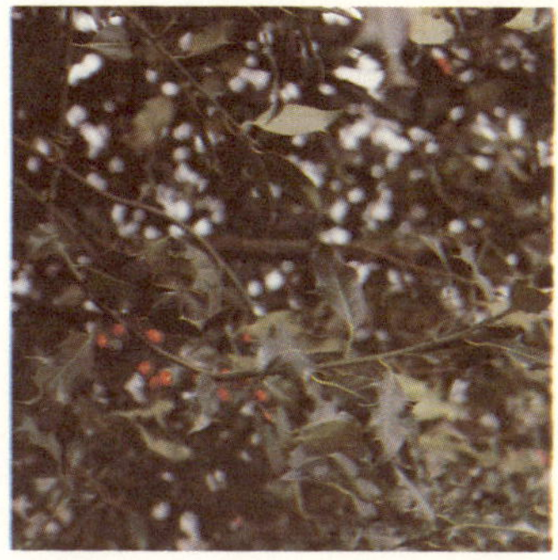

Holly △

This evergreen plant is used for hedges. The female tree will bear flowers and berries. Left unclipped, it will grow into a small tree. The berries are poisonous. The dense wood can be used for carving.

Laurel

Laurel is not a native and is grown in parks and gardens as an ornamental tree. ▽

Monkey Puzzle Tree ▷

The monkey puzzle tree is not a native of Britain, but is grown in parks and gardens as an ornamental tree. It originates from Chile. It got its English name when someone said 'it would puzzle a monkey to climb that tree'. Like the yew and the willow, monkey puzzle trees are either male or female.

Algae

The green vegetation which covers the surface of many ponds is algae, a very simple plant which contains chlorophyll. There are many forms of algae and those which live in water form the basis of an important food chain.

▽

Moss

Mosses grow in damp places. They have no flowers but instead they develop spores which, when ripe, float in the air and grow if they happen to land in a suitable place. ▽

▽

Fungi

There are many different kinds of fungi to be found growing in gardens and waste ground. Some of them are attached to wood while others grow from the ground. Although some of them may be edible they should not be touched because many of them are poisonous.

Chanterelle ▽

Wood woolly foot

Bracket Fungus △

Bracket fungus grows on trees, usually on the trunk, and is serious because it causes rot. The fungus may persist for several years. Only trees such as the yew, which has a long life span, are unaffected.

Bracket fungus hastens the decomposition of dead or dying wood.

Shaggy Ink Cap ▷

This strange fungus can be found in gardens and waste land from April until November. The gills are white at first, changing to pink and finally black.

Wild Flowers

Greater Plantain

Greater plantain was long ago known as Englishman's Foot because the seeds were carried on the clothing of early colonists. The plant is very common beside roads and in lawns.

Stinging Nettle

A very common weed with spreading roots. The square stems grow up to 1.2 m high and are covered with stinging hairs, the tips of which break off when touched, releasing an acid into the skin. The flowers are pale green and grow on trailing catkins from the bottom of the leaf stems.

During the Second World War, nettles were gathered and a green juice extracted which was used in medicines and to make green camouflage dye.

Ivy △

Ivy has two sorts of leaves. Those on the flowering stems are spear-shaped whilst those on the climbing or trailing stems have three or five lobes. The flowers appear in the autumn and the black berries, which are poisonous, develop during the winter and spring.

Broad Dock △

There are several kinds of dock, all of which have deep roots. The broad dock is very common on waste land. The leaves are supposed to lessen the pain of nettle stings if rubbed on them.

◁ *White Clover*

One of our most common plants found in lawns and waste land. The flowers bloom from May to September. After fertilisation the tiny flower heads turn brown and bend downwards.

Mugwort

60-90 cm high and found on almost any piece of waste land, mugwort is one of those plants which few people can identify. The scented leaves in the past were supposed to have magical powers. ▽

Dandelion △

The dandelion is one of our most common wild plants. Growing from a deep root, it has a rosette of long, toothed leaves and bright yellow flowers on a long stalk, followed by the seeds in a 'clock'. The flowers, which close up at night and in dull weather, can be used to make wine and the young leaves can be eaten in salad. The roots can be dried and used as a kind of coffee.

Blackberry

Although the bramble or blackberry is very common, there are many slightly different forms of the plant. The square stems send out roots whenever they touch the ground. The flowers appear from June to August, the fruit in August and September. ▽

▽

Knotgrass △

Another plant which people do not recognise. The long, slender branched stems spread along the ground or climb over other plants.

Sorrel △

This plant is common on grassland and grows to a height of 50-80cm. It has arrow-shaped leaves and a dock-like flower.

Horse Radish ▷

Often found on waste land, this is a cultivated plant which has escaped. The dock-like leaves have a tell-tale smell when rubbed. The thick root is used for flavouring food.

◁ *Cow Parsley*

Cow Parsley is also known as Wild Chervil and Queen Anne's Lace. It grows on waste land from April to June. It grows up to 1.2 m high and has hollow, slightly hairy stems.

Feverfew ▷

Although it is also known as Scentless Mayweed, the leaves have a strong smell. Long ago the plant was used as a medicine. It grows up to 60 cm high and flowers from June to September.

◁ *Shepherd's Purse*

A very common and familiar weed that is easily recognised by its triangular seed pods which are similar in shape to the purses of ancient shepherds.

◁ *White Dead Nettle*

In flower for most of the year, this plant does not sting although the leaves are similar to the stinging nettle.

Growing in clumps, it can reach a height of 60 cm.

Heartsease ▷

This tiny relative of the garden pansy can be found hiding on waste ground between much larger plants. The flowers vary in colour from yellow to purple. As its name suggests, it was once used as a heart medicine. ▷

▽

◁ *Chickweed*

The five petals of chickweed are so divided that it appears to have ten. It is a common weed found in gardens and on waste land. In a mild winter the flowers can be seen even in January.

◁ *Daisy*

The name daisy comes from 'Day's Eye' because it closes up at night. It is very common on lawns and grassy verges and is in flower throughout the year.

White Campion △

In flower from May until September, White Campion is found on waste ground, and will grow up to 90 cm in height. The stamens and leaves are hairy.

△
Ragwort ▷

This common weed, which is poisonous to cattle, is in bloom from June to October. Found on waste land, the plant has an unpleasant smell when bruised. In Scotland it is known as Stinking Willie.

Cleavers

Cleavers, also known as Goose Grass or Sticky Willie, is a straggling plant, growing over others, supporting itself by hooked bristles on its leaves and square stems. The seed pods are spread by catching on clothes and the fur of animals.

▷

Buttercup

There are several kinds of buttercup with shiny yellow flowers. Their flowers are similar but their leaves and roots differ. They all flower in spring and early summer.

▽

Rosebay Willow-herb

Growing up to 1.6 m high, it is a very common plant. It is also known as Fireweed because it is often the first plant to grow on waste land after a fire.

▽

Thistle

The common field thistle is a difficult weed because new plants can spring from small pieces of root. It grows 30-90 cm high and is found on waste land. ▷

◁ *Groundsel*

A very common garden weed which grows up to 30 cm tall. The flowers have no petals. Groundsel is often gathered as a food for cage birds.

Rayless Mayweed

Sometimes called Pineapple Weed, it is a small plant, usually less than 23 cm tall. The stalk and leaves have a strong scent. The plant grows on waste land, even if it is well trodden. ▷

◁ *Garlic Mustard*

Flowering from April to June, this plant grows by hedges or fences. The leaves smell of garlic when rubbed and they can be used in salads.

Vetch

There are many types of vetch. All of them have similar shaped flowers, for they are members of the same family. Tendrils at the end of their leaves help vetch to climb up other plants. Vetch can be found on waste land. ▽

Wild Oat (grass)

The Wild Oat can be seen in most parts of the country. It is very similar to the cultivated oat. ▽

Hops

The hop climbs by twining its rough stem in a clockwise direction. The flowers can be seen in the summer and autumn months. ▽

Herb Robert

Herb Robert has a strong unpleasant smell, but the most beautiful little deep pink flowers. The flowers grow in pairs and hang downwards at night and in bad weather. ▽

Greater Bindweed ▷

This beautiful white flower is found climbing over fences and hedges. Its stem winds in an anti-clockwise direction around other plants and supports. The flowers can be seen from June to October.

◁ *Hawkbit*

Hawkbit is related to the dandelion. The flowers and seed clocks are similar, but much smaller. Unlike the dandelion, the flower heads are found on branched stalks and the leaves are long and narrow.

Ribwort Plantain ▷

Flowering from April onwards, Ribwort is found growing on lawns, by roadsides and on waste land. If left, the plant can grow up to 60 cm high.

◁ *Red Campion*

Common in hedgerows, the flowers of Red Campion are very fragrant and attract bees. It grows to a height of 30-90 cm.

Animals and Insects

Fallow Deer △

Fallow deer are often seen in parks and woodland all over Britain. They stand about 90 cm high at the shoulder. They eat grass and weeds and the young shoots on trees. Only the males have the flattish-ended antlers which are shed every year. The antlers grow again, each time a little longer until the deer is seven years old.

△

Hedgehog ▷

Hedgehogs sleep during the day. They hunt at night for worms, snails, insects and even small creatures like mice or baby birds, or eggs. They live under heaps of twigs. When frightened, they curl up into a ball protected by their spines. In winter the hedgehog sleeps for several months.

◁ *Fox*

The fox is one of the most surprising wild animals to be found in town. Since the disease *myxomatosis* killed off so many wild rabbits, foxes can be found living near the centre of some cities where they raid dustbins and even catch cats.

The fully-grown fox is about 1.2 m long from the tip of his nose to the end of his tail.

◁ *Rat*

Once there were no rats in Great Britain. They came on ships from Asia. They are the most disliked of our wild animals for they not only carry disease, but also cause much damage.

The brown rat is about 20 cm long with a tail almost as long. It lives in sewers, rubbish tips and buildings where it can find food.

The black rat is smaller and is usually only found near ports.

◁ *House Mouse*

The house mouse is one of our smallest animals. Usually they are very shy and come out at night. They can live almost anywhere and in spite of man trapping and poisoning them they survive because they breed very rapidly and eat almost anything.

Bat

Twelve species of bats are found in Britain. They are the only flying mammals in this country.

The largest bats have bodies 10 cm long and a wingspan of 40 cm.

All our bats live on insects which they catch as they fly. They are only seen at dusk or in the early morning light. By day they sleep in old buildings and hollow trees. ▷

Grey Squirrel △

There are two kinds of squirrels in Great Britain. The red squirrel, which is a native, is very rarely seen now; it has been replaced by the bigger grey squirrel which is about 50 cm long. The grey squirrels originally came from America and were released from a zoo. They feed on berries, nuts and seeds.

Mole

These little animals live underground, but gardeners know when they are about because they push up piles of earth to form mole hills. Moles make a network of tunnels which they dig while searching for food. They eat worms, snails and insects. ▽

◁ *Frog*

After sleeping all winter, frogs lay masses of their jelly-like eggs or spawn in streams and ponds. The spawn soon hatches into tadpoles, which gradually change into frogs. First their back legs grow, then their front legs develop and their tail shrinks. Frogs grow until they are about 7-10 cm long.

Frogs live in damp, shady places and feed on worms, insects and slugs.

Newt ▷

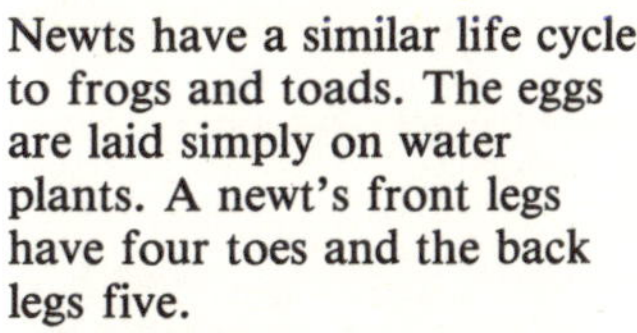

Newts have a similar life cycle to frogs and toads. The eggs are laid simply on water plants. A newt's front legs have four toes and the back legs five.

In Britain there are three species of newts; this is a Great Crested Newt.

Common Lizard

◁ The common lizard is a cold-blooded reptile which feeds on worms, insects and spiders. It is between 10 and 15 cm long and is found in all parts of Britain.

The Common Lizard does not lay eggs. Between five and ten young are born at a time.

◁ *Worm*

An earthworm's head is at the pointed end of its body. It eats soil and digests the food it contains. Worms help to break up and mix the soil.

Slug ▷

Slugs, which can be black, grey or brown in colour, are found in gardens. They feed on leaves and roots and are a nuisance to gardeners. They have a life span of up to three years.

Snail

Snails eat fresh leaves, decaying matter and even dead worms and are a nuisance in the garden. They lay round, white eggs in the soil or under stones. These hatch into tiny snails. ▽

Bumble-bee

Bumble-bees, or humble-bees as some people call them, live in colonies; they are not kept in hives but are wild. The queen, after hibernating for the winter, makes a nest in a hole or crevice.

Wasp

Wasps build their nest from a "paper" they produce from wood. Wasps feed on insects for most of the year. They only eat fruit in the autumn. Only the young queens survive the winter. Wasps, unlike bees, can sting many times.

Ant

Ants live in nests under the ground. The queen can live several years and lay many thousands of eggs. The queen and the males have wings. After mating, the queen loses her wings.

Ants, bees and wasps are insects which live in colonies, each insect having its own work within the community.

After the queen lays the eggs she is fed and cared for by the workers, who also look after the eggs and the young.

Cranefly

The cranefly is also known as the daddy-long-legs. It is quite harmless although its larvae, called leather jackets, are destructive in the garden.

Grasshopper

The grasshopper makes its familiar chirping sound by rubbing its large hind legs against its wings.

Earwig

Earwigs are insects that can be found in gardens. Under their wing cases they hide very thin wings. Unlike most insects they look after their young. They eat decaying vegetation.

Lacewing

This insect has large wings whose veins form a lacework effect. It feeds on aphids and is a great help to the gardener.

◁ *Centipede*

The centipede is a creature of dark, damp places. Its body is made up of fifteen or more segments, each with a pair of legs.

Woodlouse ▷

The woodlouse is not an insect, it is related to shrimps and lobsters. It lives under stones and pieces of wood. When in danger it curls its scaly body into a ball.

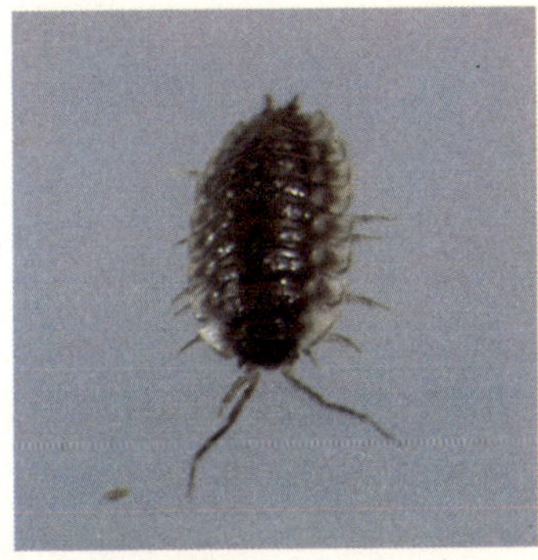

◁ *Cockroach*

Cockroaches live in warm, dark places indoors where there is food. They have small wings but cannot fly. They can run very quickly. They do not sting or bite, but have a very unpleasant smell.

Louse ▷

The louse is a parasite. It is a tiny insect that lives on the bodies of other animals. Usually one type of louse spends its whole life on one particular animal.

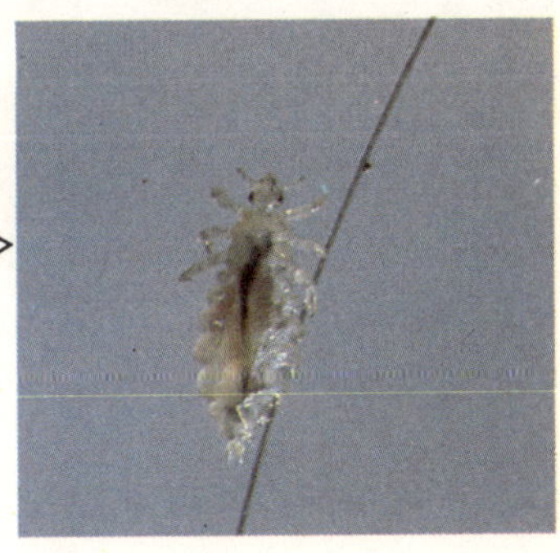

Cabbage White Butterfly

Seen in gardens from May until October, the cabbage white and small white butterflies lay their eggs upon cabbages and similar plants.

The caterpillars hatch from the eggs and feed upon the leaves until it is time for the caterpillar to turn into a chrysalis. The chrysalis gradually changes into a butterfly.

Magpie Moth

This night-flying moth has a 4 cm wingspan. The caterpillars feed on many plants: gooseberries, currants, blackthorn, heather, elm and apple. Both the moth and caterpillar have orange and black markings.

House Spider

House spiders are a reddish brown with dark markings. They make sheet-like webs in the corners of rooms, in which flies get caught. ▽

Small Tortoiseshell Butterfly

This butterfly, seen early in summer, lays its eggs on stinging nettles. In autumn it hibernates until the following spring. ▽

Garden Spider △

This dark brown spider with white markings is sometimes called the cross spider. It weaves a circular web which looks like a wheel.

Silver Fish △

These primitive insects often live in kitchens where they hide in crevices by day and come out at night to search for food scraps.

◁ *Ground Beetle*

The Violet Ground Beetle is found hiding under stones and logs. At night it comes out to hunt for other small insects, tiny creatures and decaying vegetable matter.

Blackfly and Greenfly

Blackfly and greenfly are aphids which suck the sap from the shoots of plants. They give out a sugary substance which attracts ants. They breed very fast but are eaten by birds, lacewing larvae and ladybirds. ▽

Ladybird △

The number of spots on these small red beetles can vary from two to twenty two. Ladybirds and their grubs eat greenfly and blackfly.

Birds

Robin

One of our best-loved garden birds, the robin, shows little fear of man. It is just under 15 cm long and lives on worms and insects. ▷

Great Tit

△

The Great Tit is the largest of the tit family and it is found in many gardens. It has a squeaking song and eats insects, seeds, ants and fruit.

Blue Tit

Also called the tom-tit, the Blue Tit has a shrill song. It lives near houses and often nests in a hole. The bird lives on insects, fruit and seeds. All members of the tit family are small, acrobatic birds. ▽

◁ *Blackbird*

The blackbird has a beautiful flute-like song. It eats insects, fruit and seeds. Only the male is black, the female being dark brown, sometimes with dark speckles on the throat and breast.

Thrush ▷

There are two kinds of thrushes found in our gardens. The song thrush is the more common and is about 20 cm long. The mistle thrush is bigger and has larger spots. Thrushes feed on insects, worms, berries, and snails which they break open upon a stone.

▽

Carrion Crow

Pairs of crows build their nests singly, unlike rooks whose nests are found in large groups called rookeries. Crows are large birds – up to 50 cm long – and eat insects, seeds and even small animals and birds. When on the ground the crow hops around in an ungainly manner. It has a harsh cry that sounds like 'kraak, kraak'.

▷

Rook

Smaller than the crow – about 45 cm long – the rook is found in large flocks. Rookeries are found at the tops of tall trees, more on the edges than in the centres of towns.

▷

▽

Chaffinch ▷

The Chaffinch is one of our commonest birds. It is about 15 cm long and eats insects, caterpillars and seeds. Although a resident bird, large flocks of them arrive to spend the winter here. It has a cheerful song and a call which sounds like 'chink, chink'.

◁ *House Sparrow*

The House Sparrow is seen everywhere in towns and villages. It nests under roofs and in holes in walls, or it builds a nest in trees or bushes. Sparrows do not sing but make a chirping sound.

Starling ▷

Starlings are very noisy, greedy birds and are something of a pest for they gather in large numbers and roost in towns at night. Although the starling is a resident, large flocks come to Britain every winter from Northern Europe.

Owl

Owls hunt silently at night, and during the day roost in tall trees and old buildings. Owls do not build nests but use a ledge or any convenient place. They eat small animals, birds and even insects. On the right, the Little Owl.

Kestrel

The kestrel is the most common British falcon, and sometimes nests in holes or on the ledges of tall buildings. It lives on mice and smaller birds.

Pigeon

Pigeons are very tame birds and are often found in city and town centres. They are a nuisance, for not only do they damage buildings, but damage crops in gardens. They are big birds, growing up to 40 cm in length.

▷

◁

Swan

The mute swan is grey until it is nearly three years old. One of the largest birds to be seen in the British Isles, it has a wing span of about 2.5 m. It feeds on vegetable matter found in lakes and ponds.

Mallard Duck

The mallard is the most common and well-known duck. Only the drake has a dark green head.

▽

Greylag Goose

△

The Greylag is a native of Britain, and is the ancestor of the domestic farmyard goose. It is one of only two species of wild geese to breed in Britain, the other being the Canada Goose.

Coot

△ △

The coot looks similar to a moorhen except that it is larger and has a white beak shield and no white feathers.

Canada Goose

Canada Geese are not native to the British Isles, but were introduced here from North America about 200 years ago as an ornamental bird. Like all geese it feeds on land, eating mainly grass and crops.

Swallow

Swallows live in close association with man, often relying on buildings for nesting sites.

With their long curved wings they can fly very fast and catch insects in the air.

Though they migrate to Africa, the same birds often return to the same nest year after year. The swallow is easily identified by its long forked tail, white breast and red face. They are closely related to the swift and house martin.

Wren

One of our smallest birds, the wren is only about 7 cm long. It is shy and often difficult to see.

▽

Moorhen △

About 33 cm long, the moorhen has a red beak shield and a white under-tail. It lives on snails, insects, seeds and water-weed.

◁ *Jackdaw*

The Jackdaw is the smallest member of the Crow family which includes Rooks, Jays and Magpies. It has a reputation, like the Magpie, for being a thief, as it not only robs the nests of other birds but takes and hides a variety of objects.

The Jackdaw nests high above the ground, and many buildings such as cathedrals are used as nesting sites.

It feeds in a variety of locations, from fields, with other birds such as starlings, to rubbish tips with sea-gulls.

Herring Gull

Although this is a sea bird, during the winter or in times of very bad weather it will come inland and can be seen on rubbish tips and playing fields.

Blackheaded Gulls

In winter time, blackheaded gulls fly into big cities for scraps of food and often sleep on reservoirs and lakes.

INDEX